OLD TESTAMENT STORIES

OLD TESTAMENT STORIES

RETOLD FOR CHILDREN

By
Lillie A. Faris

Author of
Standard Bible Story Readers
New Testament Stories Retold for Children

Illustrated by
W. Fletcher White

·NEW·YORK·
THE·PLATT·&·MUNK·Co INC·

Copyright MCMXL,
By
THE PLATT & MUNK CO., INC.
Made in U. S. A.

FOREWORD

FAMILIARITY with the stories of the Bible is the birthright of every child. This thought, therefore, has been kept in mind in writing these carefully selected stories for children. Stories that will make their ethical and religious impress in the finest manner.

There has been no attempt to fairyize or distort the stories. I have written them as closely as possible to the Bible text, including in each, as far as possible, the background which is true to history.

The vocabulary used is purely that of a child under twelve.

Believing as I do that it is impossible for anyone to improve upon Bible diction, a sentence or paragraph is often quoted in exact Biblical form. The language is pure, classical, and far above our poor power to improve.

So, with all the wealth of material which the Bible affords, my own part has been only to simplify words and phrases, which are beyond the child's understanding.

Stories of truth, love, courage, unselfishness, and kindness form the basis of the content of this book. With abounding love for the boys and girls who read it, it is sent on its mission.

LILLIE A. FARIS

CONTENTS

OLD TESTAMENT

	Page
NOAH AND THE ARK	13
ABRAHAM AND ISAAC	17
ISAAC AND REBEKAH	21
ISAAC'S WELLS	23
A WONDERFUL LADDER	25
A COAT OF MANY COLORS	30
FROM PRISON TO PALACE	35
A SILVER CUP	39
A FATHER AND HIS LONG LOST SON	44
A BABY IN A BASKET BOAT	47
CROSSING THE DEEP RED SEA	51
RUTH IN THE BARLEY FIELDS	55
GIDEON AND HIS BRAVE THREE HUNDRED	60
A LITTLE BOY WHO HEARD GOD'S VOICE	67
DAVID THE SHEPHERD	71
A SHEPHERD BOY AND A GIANT	75
TWO GOOD FRIENDS	80
A KING AND A LAME PRINCE	83
KING SOLOMON BUILDS A BEAUTIFUL TEMPLE	86
HOW GOD TOOK CARE OF ELIJAH	91
A CAPTIVE MAID HELPS HER MASTER	95
A GUEST ROOM	99
A LITTLE BOY KING	104
AT SCHOOL IN A KING'S PALACE	107
A FIERY FURNACE	111
IN A DEN OF LIONS	116
A QUEEN WHO SAVED HER PEOPLE	120

NOAH AND THE ARK

IN the long, long ago time, after the Father in Heaven had made the beautiful world for His children, He saw that they were becoming very wicked.

He had made the beautiful Garden of Eden, with its trees and lovely flowers and shrubs, and had placed Adam and Eve in it.

He had told them to tend the garden and that they should have everything in it to make them happy.

Adam and Eve were very happy for a long time, but they did something which God had told them not to do.

He said to them, "You will have to go away from the garden, because you have disobeyed."

Years after this, there were many people on the earth, but they did not live as God wanted them to; they were like Adam and Eve in the garden.

They seemed to think of nothing but doing evil. God was sorry that He had put men on the earth, and His heart was deeply grieved.

When He looked among the people, He found only one good man. His name was Noah.

[13]

Noah tried always to do just as God wished. He was so good, that the Bible says, "Noah walked with God."

At last, as God saw how much wrong doing there was in the world, He said, "I will destroy all the wickedness."

Then He talked to Noah, and this is what He said: "Noah, make thee an ark of gopher wood; rooms shalt thou make in the ark, and shalt pitch it within and without with pitch.

"And behold, I do bring a flood of waters upon the earth, and everything that is in the earth shall die.

"And thou shalt come into the ark, thou and thy sons, and thy wife, and thy sons' wives with thee.

"And of every living thing of all flesh, two of every sort shalt thou bring into the ark, to keep them alive with thee."

God told Noah just how the ark should be built; how long to make it, how wide and how high.

It had to be very large because all kinds of animals and birds were to live in it for many days.

It had to be very strong for it must float on the water for a long, long time.

Noah's sons helped him build the ark, and they made it exactly as God had told them.

After the ark was finished, Noah carried in the food for his family and all the animals.

Then the birds, the beasts and the creeping things went into the ark, two by two. Noah and his family followed and God shut them in

They were not afraid. They knew God would take care of them.

As soon as all were safe in the ark it began to rain; for forty days and nights it never stopped, and the water covered the whole earth.

The water was so deep that the big heavy ark floated easily upon it.

The water covered the earth for five long months and everything except the ark was swept away.

One day Noah opened the window of the ark and sent out a raven. The little bird kept flying back and forth.

Then Noah sent out a dove from the window, to see if the waters had gone down.

"But the dove found no rest for the sole of her foot, and she returned unto him into the ark, for the waters were on the face of the whole earth."

[15]

After seven days Noah sent the dove out again and this time she came back with an olive leaf in her mouth. Noah knew then that the waters were going down and the trees were rising above them.

Another week passed and Noah sent the dove out the third time. This time she did not come back at all, and he knew that she had found a place to rest and that soon the water would be gone.

One day God spoke to Noah again and said, "Go forth out of the ark, thou and thy wife, and thy sons, and thy sons' wives with thee."

Noah and his family went joyfully out of the ark and the animals followed them. Noah built an altar and offered a sacrifice, and thanked the Father in Heaven, for His great care.

While they were all at the altar, a wonderful message came from Heaven! God said, "I do set my bow in the clouds, and it shall be for a token of a covenant between me and the earth."

As Noah and his family looked up into the clouds, they saw a beautiful bow of red, orange, yellow, green, blue and violet stretched across the sky.

And God said, "This is my bow of promise. And behold, when I bring a cloud over the earth, the bow shall be seen in the cloud. And I will remember."

He set the rainbow in the sky, to show that never again would He send a flood, to cover the whole earth.

ABRAHAM AND ISAAC

MANY years after the flood there lived a man whose name was Abraham.

He was a fine old man who believed in God, and always trusted Him.

One day God spoke to Abraham. "Get thee out of thy country, and from thy kindred," He said, "and from thy father's house unto a land that I will show you."

Abraham was willing to do what God told him, and he made ready at once to leave his old home.

He did not ever ask God where He was going to send him, because God's promise had been "I will bless thee," and Abraham knew that this would be so.

He called his wife, Sarah, and his nephew, Lot, and they with their flocks of sheep and herds of cattle, set out to follow wherever the Father in heaven led them.

They had a long, long journey, but God was very kind to Abraham, and was with him all the time.

At last, after many days of travel, Abraham and his wife and nephew reached a new country, called the land of Canaan.

"This is the land which I give to thee," said God to the good old man.

Abraham built an altar and thanked God for the new home, and for all His goodness.

One day when he was sitting by his tent, under some great oak trees, he looked up and saw three angels.

These angels had come to bring Abraham good news.

They told him that before long, he and his wife would have a little boy baby of their very own.

This promise came true and the happy father and mother named their little son Isaac.

After Isaac had grown to be a fine, sturdy lad, a very hard trial came to his father.

One day he heard God's voice saying: "Abraham, take thy son Isaac, and go up into the land of Moriah, and offer him there as a burnt offering upon one of the mountains which I shall tell thee of."

Abraham did not complain. He had faith that God would care for him.

So early the next morning he and his son, Isaac, and two servants started for the land of Moriah.

It took three whole days to make the journey. When at last Abraham saw the place in the distance, he asked his servants to wait while he and Isaac went on to worship.

As Isaac watched Abraham build the altar for the offering, he was puzzled and asked, "My father, behold the fire and the wood, but where is the lamb for the burnt offering?"

"My son," said the old man, "God will provide himself a lamb." And then he bound Isaac and laid him upon the wood.

He was just ready to offer his dear son to God, when an angel called to him from heaven saying, "Abraham! Abraham!"

Abraham answered, "Here am I." Then the angel said, "Lay not thy hand upon the lad, for now I know that thou fearest God, seeing thou has not withheld thine only son."

Just as the old man looked up, he saw a ram caught in the thicket by his horns, and he took the ram and offered it as a sacrifice, instead of his own son, Isaac.

Again, the voice from heaven gave to this grand old man, the most wonderful promise that had ever been made.

The voice told Abraham that his children and his children's children, should be as many as the stars of heaven and as the sands upon the sea-shore.

God said, "In thy seed shall all the nations of the earth be blessed; because thou hast obeyed my voice."

Isaac grew up to be a loving son to Abraham and Sarah.

He was quiet and gentle and peace-loving, just as the Father in Heaven would have him.

ISAAC AND REBEKAH

WHEN Isaac had grown to be a man, his father and mother thought it was time for him to marry.

Abraham did not want Isaac to marry a woman of the new country, for he liked the women in his old home better.

One day he asked a trusty servant to go back to the old home country and choose a wife for Isaac.

The servant thought that would be a hard thing to do, but to please Abraham he set out on the long journey.

All along the way he prayed to God, to help him find the right wife for Isaac.

At last the servant reached Abraham's old home.

He stopped one evening outside a city where there was a well.

The servant knew that the women of the city, would come out to draw water. He would watch, he said to himself, for a maiden both beautiful and kind.

While he was waiting, he made the ten camels that he had brought with him, kneel down and rest.

Then the old servant spoke again to the Father in Heaven.

This was his strange prayer:

"O Lord, of my master, Abraham, I pray thee, send me good speed this day, and show kindness unto my master, Abraham.

"Behold, I stand here by the well of water, and the daughters of the men of the city come out to draw water;

"And let it come to pass, that I shall know the one thou hast appointed for Isaac, and when I say, 'Let down thy pitcher, I pray thee, that I may drink', she shall say, 'Drink, and I will give thy camels drink also.'"

Even before he had finished praying, a young girl came up to the well, her pitcher on her shoulder.

She was very fair, and as the servant looked at her, he hoped that she might be the right one.

She filled her pitcher with water, and the servant ran to meet her saying, "Let me, I pray thee, drink a little water from thy pitcher."

When he had done drinking, she said, "I will draw water for thy camels, also."

Then she drew the water for all of the camels, and the servant knew that she was the right wife for Isaac.

This fair young girl was called Rebekah.

The old servant gave her the beautiful gifts he had brought. Then he went to Rebekah's home, and asked her father if she might go back with him and become Isaac's wife.

Rebekah's father was pleased to have her go, and she and Isaac were married and lived together many happy years.

They had two children, twin boys, and they named them Jacob and Esau.

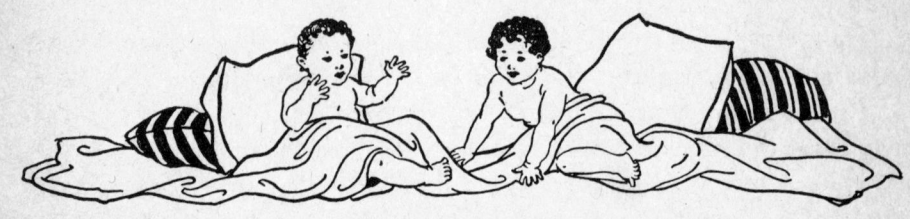

ISAAC'S WELLS

WHILE Isaac and his family, were living in the land of Canaan, a great famine came and they thought they would have to go to Egypt to get food.

But God told Isaac not to go into Egypt, but to a place called Gerar, and that he should have plenty there.

So Isaac went to Gerar, for like his father, Abraham, Isaac always did just what God asked.

Isaac was a very careful man. He took great pains with everything he did, whether it was the planting of his seed, or tending his flocks of sheep and herds of cattle.

His crops grew well and he had many sheep and cattle, and servants to care for them.

Isaac needed so much water for his sheep and cattle, that he set his herdsmen to cleaning out the wells, which his father had dug long ago.

But some of the herdsmen who lived in Gerar, wanted that water themselves, "The water is ours," they said to Isaac's men.

Isaac's servants might have quarreled with these men of Gerar about the well, but their master said to them, "Dig another."

They knew that he would not want them to quarrel, so they dug another well, and again the men of Gerar said, "The water is ours."

"Dig still another, men, we will not quarrel about water," said Isaac to his servants.

When Isaac's men dug the third well, the quarrelsome neighbors did not trouble them.

And Isaac's herdsmen were pleased, because the men of Gerar did not try to quarrel with them any more.

"There is room for us all in this land," said Isaac, "for God has been with us, and now that the men have stopped quarreling, we shall have much grain and rich pasture."

A WONDERFUL LADDER

REBEKAH and Isaac had two children. They were twins and their names were Jacob and Esau.

Jacob and Esau were just as different as day and night. Esau was a hunter, but Jacob liked to stay quietly at home, in his tent.

One day when Esau came in from the hunt, Jacob was cooking some food. It smelled very good to Esau, for he was tired and hungry.

Esau was so hungry, that he promised everything he owned to Jacob, in exchange for the food.

A long time afterwards, Esau began to think that he had done wrong to sell everything, even his birthright, to Jacob. It made him very angry to think he had been so foolish.

He vowed that he would get even with Jacob, and that some day, he would kill him.

His mother heard what Esau had said.

She called Jacob and told him that Esau had planned to kill him, and that he must go away for a while, to the home of her brother.

"You must stay there until Esau has forgiven you, then I will send for you," she said.

Rebekah did not want Isaac to know anything about the trouble between the boys, for now he was old and blind. She planned to have him send Jacob away on a different errand.

"I am afraid that Jacob will marry some girl in this country," she said to Isaac. "I wish he would go over to my brother, Laban's, and find a wife there."

Isaac called Jacob and told him to go to his uncle's country.

Then Isaac blessed him, and sent him away.

Jacob set out all alone on his long journey.

When the sun went down, he looked around for a good place to rest, for he was very tired.

At last, he found a smooth, grassy place and with a stone under his head for a pillow, and his robe around him, he lay down to sleep.

He lay there thinking of his old blind father, of his mother, and of his brother and wondering if Esau would ever forgive him, for the wrong that he had done.

By and by it grew dark all around him.

The stars came out one by one, until the whole sky seemed to be full of them.

How brightly they twinkled in the deep blue sky! But Jacob did not watch the stars long.

He was so tired that he soon fell asleep, and while he slept, he had a strange dream.

It seemed to Jacob, that there was a great ladder, reaching from earth to Heaven, and it was filled with angels.

Some of them were going up, and some were coming down, and at the very top of the ladder, stood God Himself.

He said to Jacob, "I am the Lord God of Abraham, thy father, and the God of Isaac: the land whereon thou liest, to thee will I give it, and to thy seed.

"Behold, I am with thee, and will keep thee. I will bring thee again to this land, for I will not leave thee."

In the morning when Jacob awoke, he could not get the dream out of his mind.

He could still see the angels, he could see the great ladder reaching from earth to Heaven, and he could hear God's voice, telling him that He had given him all that beautiful country, for himself and for his children after him.

"Surely," said Jacob, "God is in this place, and this is the house of God, and this is the gate of Heaven."

He got up very early and took the stone, which had been his pillow and set it up for an altar, and poured oil upon the top of it.

Then he named the place Bethel, and made this vow:

"If God be with me in this way that I go, and will give me bread to eat, and raiment to put on, so that I may come again to my father's house in peace, and Jehovah will be my God;

"Then the stone, which I have set up for a pillar, shall be God's house: and of all that thou shalt give me, I will surely give a tenth unto thee."

Jacob went on to his uncle Laban's home and stayed there for a great many years.

He worked for his uncle Laban, and he himself became very rich.

After a long time, he planned to take his family and go back home.

He was not sure what his brother might do, but you will be glad to know, that Esau was willing to forgive all the wrong that Jacob had done.

Esau was so happy to have him come back home, that he took four hundred men and went out to meet Jacob.

When Jacob and his family drew near, Esau ran to greet his brother and flung his arms around him. Their quarrels were over.

Jacob had brought Esau many gifts, for now he was a rich man.

But Esau said, "I have enough, my brother. Let that which thou hast be thine."

At last, however, Esau took the gifts to please Jacob.

"Come now, let's be going," said Esau after a time, "I will go on before you," but Jacob said, "We cannot go as fast as you may want to.

"The children are young and there are little lambs that cannot travel very fast. Go on, and we will follow you more slowly."

Esau kindly offered to leave some of his men behind to help, but Jacob did not need them.

Jacob and his family took their time and rested along the way. After a while, they reached the place, Bethel, where Jacob had seen the wonderful ladder, that reached from earth to Heaven.

A COAT OF MANY COLORS

LONG, long ago, there was a man named Jacob. He was a rich man and had great herds of cattle and flocks of sheep. Jacob had twelve sons.

His older sons tended his sheep and cattle, but the younger ones, Joseph and Benjamin, stayed at home with their father.

Joseph had always been a good boy, and his father was very glad indeed, to have him stay at home.

Benjamin was such a little boy, that he could not be of any help at all in the pasture.

The old father loved all his boys dearly, but it seemed that he loved Joseph best of all.

One day Jacob took a piece of beautiful cloth of many colors, green, blue, red and yellow, and made Joseph a coat.

Joseph was delighted with his new coat and proudly showed it to everyone in the family.

The brothers were very jealous, when they saw their father's beautiful gift to Joseph.

They had ugly thoughts in their hearts, and they said many unkind things about Joseph and their father.

Sometimes Joseph had strange dreams.

Once he dreamed that he and his brothers, were all out in the field where the grain was ripe, and they were cutting and binding it into sheaves.

It seemed to Joseph that his sheaf stood up straight, and that the sheaves of his brothers were bowing to his own.

The brothers were angry when Joseph told them his dream. They were afraid it meant that Joseph would some day, rule over them. After that they would not even speak kindly to him.

At last they decided they would get even with Joseph in some way, and they kept watch all the time, to see how they might catch him.

Once when they were tending the cattle and sheep, they saw that there was very little green left in the pasture, so they moved on to another.

This pasture was a long way from their old home.

When some time had passed, Jacob was anxious to know how his sons were getting along, and he sent Joseph to find out.

After a long journey Joseph came in sight of the field, where they had been first.

He met a man who told him, that his brothers had moved away, to another far away pasture.

Some boys would have turned around and gone home, but not Joseph. His father had sent him to find out about the boys, so he went straight on.

At last, in the distance he saw the flocks of sheep.

He was very glad to know that he had found his brothers, and hurried on as fast as he could.

The brothers saw him coming across the fields, and they began to plan to get rid of him.

They were still very jealous of him and afraid that some day, he might be their ruler.

"Here comes the Dreamer," said one of them, "let's take him and kill him, and tell our father that a wild beast did it."

But Reuben, another brother said, "Let us not take his life; cast him into this pit, but lay no hand upon him."

Reuben thought, that if Joseph were put in the pit, later on, when his brothers were not looking, he could pull him out and send him safely back home.

Reuben had to go to another part of the field, to see about some of the sheep.

While he was gone, his brothers sat down to eat their lunch.

As they were eating, one of them happened to look up and saw a long line of camels, winding down the path.

An evil thought came into his mind. He said to the rest, "Look! there are merchants going down into Egypt, with their great loads of spices. Maybe we can get them to buy Joseph."

"They could sell him as a slave down there; we could make some money, and we'd never be troubled with him again."

The others thought that this was a good idea.

So when the merchants came up, they asked them if they would buy a boy and take him to Egypt, to sell as a slave.

After a time the men made a bargain, and the brothers sold Joseph, for twenty pieces of silver.

Then the brothers took Joseph out of the pit, stripped off his beautiful coat of many colors, and sent him away with the merchants.

Away, away went the camels, and before long they were out of sight.

And away, away went Joseph!

Back in the field the older brother Reuben, was planning how he would take Joseph out of the pit, when the others were not looking and send him back home. He went to the pit, and looked inside. No Joseph was there!

Reuben was so troubled, that he cried aloud.

He ran to his brothers saying, "The child is not; and I, whither shall I go?"

Then they told Reuben what they had done with Joseph.

"See," said they, "here is his coat; we are going to kill a goat and dip this in its blood, then we'll take the coat home to father."

The brothers took the beautiful coat and dipped it in the blood, and said to their old father, "This have we found; know now whether it be thy son's coat, or not."

Jacob knew that it was Joseph's coat, and he said, "It is my son's coat; an evil beast hath devoured him."

Then the poor old father mourned for his son many days.

He never dreamed that Joseph might be alive and that he might some day, see him again.

FROM PRISON TO PALACE

AFTER the merchants had reached Egypt, they sold Joseph to a captain, who wanted Joseph to work in his own home.

One day the captain's wife told some wicked stories about Joseph, and, though they were not true, Joseph was put into prison.

Joseph was in prison for a long, long time, and while he was there, he made friends with all of the other prisoners.

The prisoners were very kind to Joseph and learned to love him dearly.

Even the man who kept the prison loved and trusted Joseph, and showed him many favors.

Sometimes the men would have strange dreams and God gave Joseph the power to tell their meaning.

The king's baker and the king's butler, were both in the prison, and each had a strange dream.

The dreams troubled the men very greatly, and they asked Joseph what their dreams meant.

Joseph told them and the dreams came true, exactly as he said.

The king of that country had a strange dream also, and he sent for all the wise men and magicians in his country to explain it, but they could not.

One day, the king's butler went before him and bowed very low, saying, "Oh, king, there is a young man in the prison, who can tell you the meaning of your dream."

"Two years ago I had a very strange dream and he told me the meaning of it; and every word came true. Send for him, oh king."

The king listened to his butler and sent for Joseph to come to the palace.

As soon as Joseph received the king's message, he put on his best clothes and went to the palace.

The king was pleased when this neatly dressed young man stood before him.

He said, "I have sent for you because I have been told that you can tell the meaning of dreams, and I have had a very strange one.

"I dreamed that I stood by a river side; and behold, there came up out of the river, seven cattle that were fat and well kept; and behold, seven lean cattle came up and stood by the seven fat cattle.

"After a while the seven lean cattle ate up the seven fat cattle.

"Now Joseph, can you tell me what this dream means? There is nobody in all my kingdom who can."

Joseph told the king that it was God's power, that had helped him to tell the meaning of dreams, and that he would do the best he could.

Then he told the king that the seven fat cattle, meant that there would be seven years of plenty, and the seven lean cattle, showed that there would be seven years of famine. He said, "Oh king, God hath declared to you, what He is about to do.

"You and all your people, must plan to build great barns and storehouses, so that you can take care of all the grain that grows in the seven years of plenty."

Then Joseph gave the king another message from God, that he must look for a man who would be wise and strong, to take care of this work.

The king asked Joseph to be his helper; he said, "You are the wisest man in the kingdom." He gave Joseph beautiful clothes to wear and a fine chariot.

Then he sent Joseph out among the people, to ask them to take care of all the grain, and to get ready for the great famine which was to come.

As Joseph rode around among the people in his beautiful chariot, they cried to one another, "Bow the knee!" and all the people bowed to Joseph, because he was a very great man,—the greatest in all their land, except the king himself.

All the time that Joseph had been in prison God was with him. He had helped Joseph to do right in all things.

Joseph never forgot to thank God for His help.

A SILVER CUP

THE king of Egypt was well pleased with Joseph, because he was so wise and good.

The people liked him, too, for his kindness to them.

There were times, however, when Joseph felt very sad.

He often thought of his old father Jacob, far away in the land of Canaan, and wondered why no message had ever come to him.

He never once thought that his brothers would make his father believe that he was dead.

After Joseph had been in Egypt a good many years, and all the big barns and storehouses were filled with food, the famine came in earnest.

It spread all over the land, even to Joseph's old home.

In some way the people throughout the whole country learned, that there was plenty of food in Egypt. They had heard of the good wise man, who had told them that the famine was coming and that they must get ready for it.

They heard, too, that the people in Egypt would share their corn, with all the countries around them just as long as it lasted.

Many made the trip to far away Egypt to buy the food they needed.

One day Jacob said to his sons, "Go over to the land of Egypt and buy corn."

So the ten older brothers started out on the long journey, but Jacob was afraid to have Benjamin, the younger son, go so far away.

When Joseph's brothers reached the land of Egypt, they went before the great new ruler to buy their corn, but they did not know Joseph. Joseph, however, knew his brothers and asked them many questions.

He said, "You are spies, and you have come over here to see the nakedness of the land." "Nay, my lord," answered the brothers, "we are come to buy food.

"We are all one man's sons and we are true men. We are not spies."

But Joseph told them that they would have to prove that they were all sons of one man and that they had a young brother at home.

He told them to leave one of the brothers there, and go back home for their youngest brother. If they did this, no harm would come to them.

There was nothing in the world Joseph wanted so much, as to see his old father and his young brother, Benjamin.

He was trying to plan some way by which he could have them all come over to Egypt.

When he was ready for his brothers to go back, he told his men to fill the bags with grain and to put all their money back into the sacks. When the brothers reached home and opened the bags, there lay the money in the top of each one.

After a long time they had to go back to Egypt for more corn, but they knew it would be no use to go, without Benjamin.

They told their father what the great ruler had said to them, and at last he allowed Benjamin to go.

When Joseph saw his brothers coming back with Benjamin, he ordered servants to cook a fine dinner for them.

Joseph welcomed his brothers joyfully. He asked about their father. When he saw Benjamin he asked, "Is this your youngest brother, of whom you spoke to me?"

Then turning to Benjamin he said, "God be gracious to thee, my son."

Joseph wanted to put his arms around the brother he had longed to see, but he did not dare to before the others, for fear they would guess who he was. So he went out of the room to hide his feelings.

After a while they all sat down to dinner and feasted happily. Joseph had thought of a way to keep his youngest brother with him.

He sent for his servant and said, "Fill the men's sacks with as much food as they can carry, put all the money back into their sacks again."

Then he took his own beautiful silver cup and said, "Put this silver cup into the sack that belongs to the youngest."

As soon as it was light enough the next morning, the brothers started on their way home.

Then Joseph called his servant and said, "Up and after the men and tell them my silver cup is gone."

"Tell them that the one in whose sack it is found, shall be my bondsman."

The brothers were frightened, when the servant told them to look for the silver cup.

All the men untied their sacks and the cup was found in Benjamin's.

The brothers did not know what to do, for they had promised their father, that they would surely take good care of Benjamin.

One of them, named Judah, begged hard that Benjamin be allowed to go back home.

He told Joseph all the promises they had made their father about Benjamin. "We cannot go home:" he said, with tears in his eyes, "if our youngest brother be not with us, for our father will surely die."

Joseph saw that he could not let his brothers go back home, without telling them the truth, so he sent all his servants out of the room.

He cried aloud, and said to his brothers, "I am your brother Joseph. Doth my father yet live?"

The brothers were very much ashamed of themselves. They fell on their knees before Joseph and begged his forgiveness.

He told them not to grieve, for his life was just as God had planned it.

"It was His way to send me here, to save you from the famine," he said.

"Go back to my father and tell him that I am alive and that he must come here to live.

"You must tell him all that you have seen and you must all come back with him, and bring your wives and children."

A FATHER AND HIS LONG LOST SON

THERE was great excitement in the king's palace, when the servants found out that the strange men were Joseph's brothers.

The king himself was as pleased as anyone, and he sent for Joseph to come to him.

"Have your brothers load their beasts with food and go back to the land of Canaan after your father and their families," said he.

"Tell them to bring them here to live and they shall have the best of the land."

So Joseph went to his brothers and gave them the king's message.

He told them that the famine would last five years longer, and that they could come to live in Egypt and have everything they needed.

"Bring your families," he said, "and everything you have; your sheep and cattle and servants."

When they were ready for the long journey home, he loaded his brothers with presents and he sent a lovely gift to his dear father, Jacob.

Over in the land of Canaan the good old father, was watching for his boys to come back.

One evening as he sat in front of his tent, he caught sight of a long line of camels and wagons winding along the road. When they drew near he was surprised and delighted to see his own sons.

How happy the good old man was, when his sons told him that Joseph was still alive, and that he was governor over all the land of Egypt!

At first he could not believe what they said; they told him how kind Joseph had been to them, and they gave him the fine present he had sent.

Jacob said, "It is enough; Joseph my son is yet alive. I will go to see him before I die."

Just as soon as it was possible, Jacob and his sons and their wives and families, got ready to go.

The children were all very happy and talked about their uncle Joseph, and the presents he had sent them.

A beautiful thing happened to the old grey haired man, just before he started into Egypt.

God sent a vision to him, and His voice said, "Jacob, I am the God of thy fathers. Do not be afraid to go down into Egypt, for I will make a great nation of thee."

Jacob was sure then, that his journey would be a safe one.

Many people along the way stopped their work and went out to watch Jacob and his sons, as they left the home country of Canaan and went over to Egypt.

Some of them had been Jacob's good friends and they knew they would never see him again.

Just as soon as Joseph knew that his father was on the way, he started out to meet him.

It had been more than twenty years since Joseph had seen his father, so you can imagine how happy the meeting was.

They put their arms about each other and stood and cried for joy.

After a while they went up to the king's palace and Joseph took his father by the hand, and said, "Oh king, this is my father, Jacob."

The two men began to talk to each other, and the king asked Jacob how old he was.

"I am a hundred and thirty years old," answered Jacob.

Jacob lifted up his hands and blessed the king and went away with Joseph.

Joseph showed his father and brothers the rich land that was to be theirs.

"The king says that you may take your choice of all the land here," he told them, "and use it for yourselves, your flocks and your herds."

Jacob lived in the land of Goshen, near Egypt with Joseph and his other sons and their boys and girls for seventeen long and happy years.

A BABY IN A BASKET BOAT

MANY years after Joseph lived in the country of Egypt, a new king ruled there, who was very selfish and cruel.

There were in Egypt at this time, many people who had come there to get food, when there was a famine in their own beautiful land.

They stayed on and on, year after year, until there were thousands and thousands of them.

The king made them work as slaves and had them beaten, when they did not work hard enough to please him.

He would look at them and say, "These people of Israel are very strong and getting stronger every day.

"Soon they will be greater than my own people, and perhaps they will want to take my country.

"I must think of some way, to keep them from growing so mighty."

At last he thought of a plan. "I will kill all the little boy babies," said the king, "then there will not be so many men."

The king sent for his soldiers and said to them, "Men, these people of Israel are getting too strong for us.

"Go out among their tents and wherever you find a boy baby, throw him in the river."

In one of the tents there lived a man and a woman, who had a little son and daughter and a beautiful brown-eyed baby boy.

"The king's soldiers must not get my dear little baby boy," said the anxious mother.

She hid him away safely for three months, but both she and her husband knew, that some day the king would find out about their baby. The child was getting old enough now, to laugh and crow. And like all healthy babies, he often cried very hard.

What if a soldier or one of the king's people should pass by their tent and hear him!

Day and night the mother thought of nothing, but how she might save her baby.

One day she said to her little daughter, "Miriam, I believe I have thought of a way."

Taking little Miriam with her, the mother went down to the river bank and gathered long grasses and bulrushes. She wove them in and out in the shape of a basket, just big enough to hold her baby.

Then she daubed the basket all over with mud and pitch. This was to keep the water out, for the basket was to be a little boat, for her baby boy.

She worked very hard and little Miriam helped, too.

At last the little boat was ready and the mother tucked her baby snugly inside and laid it among the rushes by the river bank.

She chose the place where the princess, the daughter of the king, came every day to bathe.

She hoped that if the Princess once saw her beautiful baby, she would want to keep him and care for him.

She gave the baby a goodbye kiss and told little Miriam to hide in the bushes and see what happened.

Miriam went back among the tall grasses and hid where she could see everything.

She did not have very long to wait, for down the path came the princess and her maids.

As the princess stepped down to go into the water, she saw the strange looking little boat and sent a maid to bring it to her.

Miriam's heart beat very fast as she lay hidden in the bushes, for she did not know whether the princess would be pleased or angry.

The maid carried the basket to her mistress and opened it. The baby looked up at the princess with his big brown eyes and seeing a stranger instead of his own mother, he began to cry.

The princess saw what a fine child he was and she felt sorry for him. She knew at once that he must be a little Hebrew baby, but she did not want any harm to come to the poor, helpless little fellow.

When Miriam saw that the princess had a kind heart, she ran to her and said, "Princess, do you want a nurse to take care of this baby for you? Shall I go and call a nurse?"

And when the princess answered, "Go," she ran for her own mother.

She was very happy that her baby brother was safe, and she ran as fast as she could.

"Oh mother," she cried, "the princess wants a nurse for the baby."

The mother hurried to the princess.

"Take this child away," said she, "and nurse it for me, and I will give thee thy wages." And she put the baby into the arms of his own mother.

How happy the baby's mother was to be able to care for her own little boy, until he was big enough to go to the princess' home.

Nobody dared kill him now, for he belonged to the princess.

When the baby was big enough, the mother took him to the king's palace, and gave him to the princess.

"I shall call his name Moses," said she, "because I drew him out of the water."

CROSSING THE DEEP RED SEA

MOSES, the little boy baby, that the king's daughter had found by the river side, grew up to be a man.

He had lived in the king's palace and been treated like a prince, yet in some way, he seemed to know that he did not belong to the princess' people, but that he was a Hebrew—one of the slave people.

The people of Egypt were cruel to these Hebrews, and one day when Moses was out walking, he saw one of his own people get a very hard beating.

Moses could not bear to see his countrymen so badly treated. He struck the cruel man of Egypt and killed him.

Moses knew that he could no longer stay in Egypt, so he left the palace and traveled far away into another country.

There he lived for a great many years.

One day when he was out watching the sheep, he saw something very strange.

A bush that was standing by the roadside, was all aglow with fire, yet it did not burn up.

There, from the midst of the burning bush, came a voice saying, "Moses, Moses!"

It was God's voice speaking.

He told Moses that he had seen, how cruelly his people were treated in Egypt and how unhappy they were there. He had chosen Moses, He said, to go back to Egypt and lead them to a beautiful new land, a land flowing with milk and honey.

Now it had been forty years since Moses had killed the cruel man of Egypt, yet he was still afraid to go back. But God promised His help saying, "Certainly I will be with thee."

Then God told Moses exactly what he wanted him to do and showed him, just how everything should be done.

Moses was an old man of eighty, but he bravely journeyed back to Egypt, to lead his people to the promised land.

It took Moses a long time to get everything ready, in the way God had planned but at last, after many hardships, all of his people started for the land of Canaan, their new home.

God had promised to put a beautiful cloud in the sky, to go before them by day to be their guide. When the cloud stopped, they must stop.

And at night God gave them a pillar of fire, like a great torch. He said, whenever the pillar of fire stopped, they must stop.

As the cloud led the way by day and the pillar of fire by night the people followed. After a while they came to a great sea.

Now, when the king of Egypt heard that Moses had led the people of Israel out of the land, he was sorry to have lost all his hard working slaves.

"Let us follow and bring them back," he cried.

He jumped into his own chariot and ordered his captains to follow with hundreds more chariots, and they all galloped away at full speed, to overtake the people of Israel.

As Moses' people, in their camp by the sea saw the king's army coming, with its hundreds of horses and chariots, they were very much afraid.

Even before this, though Moses was trying his best to help them, they had found a great deal of fault with him. Now they turned to Moses with ugly words:

"Why did you take us away?" they said. "It were better for us to stay there, than to come up here and die."

But Moses without losing his temper in the least, tried to calm and comfort them. "Fear ye not;" he said, "stand still and see what Jehovah will do for you today. Jehovah will fight for you, and ye shall hold your peace."

Then God told Moses to lift up his rod and stretch his hand out over the sea.

When Moses lifted up his rod and stretched out his hand over the sea, the water divided.

Then God made a strong wind blow all night long, to hold the sea back, so that there was a path of dry land through it.

Moses and the people crossed the sea on dry land, with the waters like a wall on either side of them.

Behind them came the king and his army. They saw the path of dry land through the sea and started across, after the people of Israel.

When the king's soldiers were out in the middle of the sea, God took off their chariot wheels, and they were very much frightened.

"Jehovah fighteth for *them*, let us flee from the face of Israel," they said.

Then God spoke to Moses, "Stretch thy hand over the sea, that the waters may come again upon the Egyptians, upon their chariots and upon their horsemen."

Moses stretched out his hand and the waters came rushing back and all the king's soldiers were destroyed.

After that, the people of Israel knew that God was taking care of them, and they believed in Him and in Moses.

RUTH IN THE BARLEY FIELDS

ONCE a happy family of four people lived in the quaint little town of Bethlehem. The father's name was Elimelech and the mother's, Naomi. There were two boys, Mahlon and Chilion.

They were all happy and contented, until one year no rain fell and nothing would grow in the land.

So they had to move far away into another country.

This country was called Moab and the people were called Moabites.

Mahlon and Chilion made many new friends, among the Moabite boys and girls, and they grew to manhood there.

Not very long after they had moved into this new country, the father was taken sick and died.

Naomi was left alone with her two boys. They were good sons in every way, but she was often very lonely.

One day Mahlon and Chilion told their mother, that they wished to marry and bring their two beautiful Moabite brides home, to be her daughters.

Naomi wanted her boys to be happy, so she gladly welcomed her two new daughters-in-law, Orpah and Ruth.

The young people all tried to make her cheerful, and she forgot part of her sorrow, when she thought of her children's happiness.

They were not happy for very long, however, because another very great sorrow came to Naomi. Her two boys fell sick and died, and again, the little home in Moab was sad.

Orpah and Ruth were just as lonely as she was.

Naomi often thought now of her old home in Bethlehem and longed to go back to her friends there.

One day some news came from home.

There had been very much rain there and the wheat and barley were growing well. There was plenty of other food, too.

Naomi felt that she must go back.

The girls helped her to get together her few belongings and went along to see her safely on her way.

They were willing to go all the way with her, but Naomi told them that they would be much happier among their own people, and she begged them to go back.

Orpah did not need much coaxing; she loved Naomi but she was not sure she would be happy in the new country, so at last, she kissed Naomi goodbye and turned back home.

After Orpah had gone Naomi said to Ruth, "Behold, thy sister-in-law is gone back to her people, and unto her Gods: return thou after thy sister-in-law."

But Ruth put her arms around Naomi and said to her, "Entreat me not to leave thee, and to return from following after thee.

"For whither thou goest, I will go; and where thou lodgest, I will lodge; thy people shall be my people, and thy God my God; where thou diest will I die, and there will I be buried."

Naomi was glad, that Ruth loved her dearly enough, to leave her own land for her sake. So the two went on their way and, at last, the long journey was ended.

When they came to Bethlehem, Naomi saw that all her neighbors and friends were very busy in the barley fields.

The fields had never looked prettier to her;—they were full of waving, heavy grain.

In those days farmers did not have machines for reaping.

They cut the grain with long knives, and piled it upon their arms.

Of course some of it always fell to the ground. Anyone who wanted to pick this up, was allowed to keep it.

Picking up the grain that the reapers had dropped, or gleaning as it was called, was work that Ruth could do. It seemed to her a good way to help Naomi.

So Ruth followed the reapers and gathered the barley they dropped. When evening came, she had almost a bushel of the grain.

One day when she was hard at work, Boaz, the rich man who owned the field, saw her and asked his workman who she was.

He was told that she was Naomi's daughter-in-law, from the land of Moab, and that she worked hard and carried all the grain home to Naomi.

Boaz gave orders to the men in his field, to let plenty of grain drop so that Ruth might have it.

One day he spoke to Ruth; "Do not go to any other field to glean. I've told these men here to treat you well."

Ruth bowed low before him and said, "Why are you so kind to me seeing that I am a stranger?"

Then Boaz told her, that he knew how good she was to Naomi and he asked God's blessing upon her.

"May God repay you for your work, and reward you, for you have taken refuge under His wings," he said.

That evening when Ruth went home, she was very happy to tell Noami about the rich man, who had been so kind to her.

Then she learned that he was Noami's kinsman.

Sometime after this Ruth and Boaz were married and lived very happily in Bethlehem.

When you read about the great king, David, you may like to know that Ruth was his great grandmother.

GIDEON AND HIS BRAVE THREE HUNDRED

BEFORE the days of threshing machines, men spread the wheat stalks on the floor and beat the grain from the hulls.

One day, when a young man named Gideon was beating the wheat, an angel from heaven came and sat down under a great oak tree nearby.

The angel saw how well Gideon worked; and saw too, what a fine, strong young man he was.

The angel had brought a message to this young man, from God in Heaven.

"Jehovah is with thee, thou mighty man of valor," said the angel to Gideon, but Gideon answered, "Jehovah hath cast us off.

"Our fathers have told us how He brought us across the Red Sea, but He has surely forsaken us now."

Gideon had a reason for making this answer.

For seven years, a people called the Midianites had been stealing everything they could get from the Israelites, their cattle and sheep, their wheat and barley.

Even while Gideon had been threshing, he had wondered where

he could hide his wheat, to be safe from the thieving hands of the Midianites.

He thought God could no longer be with the Israelites or He would protect them from the Midianites.

But Gideon did not know that God had been using the Midianites, as a punishment for his people.

After He had taken His own people, from their lives of slavery in Egypt and brought them safely across the Red Sea, into the promised land, they had been careless about keeping His laws.

They had done so many wicked things that God said, "My people no longer care for My commands; perhaps if they get into trouble again, they will come back and ask My help, and I will save them."

Gideon was greatly surprised, when the angel gave him the rest of God's message: "Go in thy might, and save Israel from the hands of the enemy, have I not sent thee?"

But Gideon felt that he was just a poor young man and his father's tribe was the poorest of all, and he said, "How can *I* save Israel? I am the least in my father's house."

The same comforting answer that God had given to Abraham,

and to others came to Gideon: "Surely I will be with thee, and thou shalt smite the Midianites."

Gideon bade the angel to give him some sign, that it was really God talking to him.

"Stay here, I pray thee," he said, "until I come and bring thee a present." And the angel answered, "I will tarry until thou come."

Then Gideon went inside the tent. He cooked some goat meat and made some little cakes of bread.

Then he carried a basket of meat and cakes and a pot of broth, to the angel waiting under the oak tree.

"Put the cakes and the flesh on this rock, and pour the broth over them," said the angel, and Gideon did so.

Then the angel put the end of the staff on the flesh and the cakes, and fire came up and burned them. And when Gideon looked up, the angel was gone.

Now Gideon knew, that the message had really come from God. Meanwhile the Midianites were making ready to fight.

Gideon wanted to be sure that God would help him, before he went out against them.

"Oh Jehovah," he said to God, "I will put a piece of wool on the threshing floor, and if there be dew on the fleece only, and dry on all the ground, then shall I know that thou wilt save Israel by my hand."

On the next morning, when Gideon went out to see the fleece of wool, it was so wet that he wrung out a whole bowlful of water.

Gideon was so poor and humble, that he could hardly believe that God had chosen him, and once again he prayed.

He said, "O Lord, do not be angry with me, but let me make another trial with this fleece; let it now be dry only upon the fleece and upon all the ground let there be dew."

In the morning when Gideon went back to the fleece, he found it perfectly dry, but the ground was covered with dew.

There was no doubt in Gideon's mind now—he was sure that God was with him, and he called a great army of the people together.

There were about thirty-two thousand of them and they camped by a stream of water which flowed from a spring.

Away to the north of them were thousands and thousands of Midianites ready to fight.

God did not want Gideon to have so many men, and He told

him that if anyone was afraid he might go home. Twenty-two thousand of them went.

That left ten thousand to do the fighting. But God wanted the people to know that He was helping them, and that He did not even need ten thousand.

He said to Gideon, "The people are yet too many; bring them down to the water and I will try them for you there."

Then God said, "When the people go to drink, some of them will lap the water like a dog; some of them will kneel down to drink.

"Put all the men that lap water like a dog in one place, and put all those that get down on their knees to drink, in another place."

When the men were tried out, there were three hundred that dipped the water in their hands and put it to their mouths and lapped.

The others got down on their knees and drank.

It was easy to see, that the men who dipped the water in their hands and put it to their mouths could work faster, than those who got down on their knees to drink, and they were the ones that God chose to go with Gideon.

The other men were sent back to their tents, and that very night God told Gideon what to do next.

"Arise," He said, "go down into the camp, and you shall hear what they say."

Gideon and his servant went down into the camp, where most of the Midianites were sleeping.

But there were some men awake, and Gideon and his servant overheard, one man telling a dream to another.

"I have had a dream," he said, "I dreamed that a cake of barley bread tumbled into our camp and hit the tent so hard, that it turned upside down and fell flat."

"This is nothing else save the sword of Gideon;" the other answered, "for into his hand hath God delivered all our people."

Gideon went back to his camp at once and divided the three hundred men into companies.

He gave each man a trumpet and an empty pitcher, with a torch inside of it.

"When we get outside their camp," said Gideon to his men, "do as I do; when I blow the trumpet, you do the same."

The three companies went over to the camp of the Midianites; they watched their leader and when Gideon gave the order, they blew the trumpets and broke the pitchers.

They held their torches high in their left hands, and they held their trumpets in their right hands, and they all cried out, "The sword of the Lord and of Gideon!"

The Midianites awoke from their sleep; they did not know that there were only a few men attacking them; they thought there were thousands.

They saw the light of the torches; they heard the awful words, "The sword of the Lord and of Gideon," and they ran away as fast as they could.

God had saved His own chosen people once again, and the Midianites gave them no more trouble.

A LITTLE BOY WHO HEARD GOD'S VOICE

THERE was once a good woman whose name was Hannah. She tried to do right at all times, and once every year she and her husband went to pray in God's temple, at a place called Shiloh.

Hannah was very sad because she had no children and as she went about her work day after day, she made up her mind to ask God to send her a little boy.

When she went up to Shiloh to the temple, she prayed to God and said, "Oh Jehovah, if You will give me a little son, I will surely give him unto Jehovah all the days of his life."

And the good priest, Eli, saw her praying there.

By and by God answered Hannah's prayer and gave her a little boy.

She and her husband named the child Samuel, and they gave him the best of care that he might grow big and strong.

Just as soon as he was old enough, Hannah took little Samuel up to the temple and said to the good priest, Eli, "I am the woman who prayed here in the temple for God to give me a little boy.

"I promised God that I would give the child to Him, and so, today, I have brought him to stay here in the temple with you."

Then Hannah knelt down in the temple, and thanked God for the little boy whom He had sent.

Hannah left Samuel in the temple and went back home.

The good old priest, Eli, taught Samuel the ways of the temple and the little boy tried his best to do everything that Eli told him.

Back at home as Hannah went about her work, she thought often of the little boy she had given to God.

Every year she made him a little coat, and took it with her when she went up to pray in God's temple.

She always tried to find the finest cloth and to make the coat as neatly as possible.

Samuel's room was in the temple, and one night as he lay on his little bed, he heard a voice say, "Samuel, Samuel."

The little boy answered, "Here am I," and ran into Eli's room.

"Here am I," he said to Eli, "for thou calledst me." But Eli said, "I called not, my son; lie down again."

Samuel went back to his room and lay down, but very soon he heard the voice again, "Samuel, Samuel."

Again Samuel ran to Eli and said, "Here am I, for thou calledst me."

But Eli told him once more, that he had not called and that he must go back to his room and lie down.

The same thing happened a third time and then Eli understood that God had called the child.

The old priest explained to Samuel, that it was God's voice that he had heard. And he told him if God should call again, to answer Him this way: "Speak, Lord, for thy servant heareth."

Samuel went back to bed and it was not very long before he heard the voice again.

"Speak, Lord, for thy servant heareth," the boy answered just as Eli had told him.

Then God gave Samuel a message about Eli's sons.

He was very much displeased with them because they had been very wicked.

In the morning Samuel was afraid to tell Eli what had happened, but Eli called him and asked, "What is this thing that the Lord has said unto thee?"

Then Samuel told Eli everything that God had said.

The old priest was very sad, but he said, "It is the Lord: let Him do what seemeth Him good."

Samuel grew to be a great strong man, and every time God spoke to him, he obeyed.

After he grew older, he became one of the great judges of Israel, and when the people asked for a king, Samuel was the messenger that God sent to annoint him.

It was he who poured the oil on the head of Saul, the first king of the people of Israel.

It was Samuel who anointed David, when he was to become the king.

After Samuel had grown very old, he stood before all the people of Israel and told them that he had always tried to do right and obey the Father in heaven.

He told them, that if they would try to live close to God, He would always take care of them.

The people all knew that Samuel was a good man, and they asked him to pray for them.

Samuel promised that he would, and when he had urged them and their king always to be true to God, he bade them goodbye.

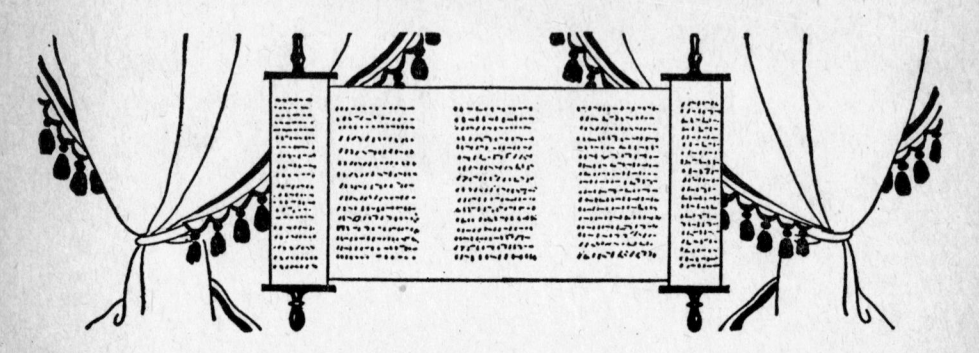

DAVID THE SHEPHERD

ONCE upon a time there lived, in the town of Bethlehem, a Jewish boy named David. His father, Jesse, owned great flocks of sheep and herds of cattle.

There were no fences around the fields near Bethlehem, so shepherds had to watch the flocks, to keep them from straying away.

When the boys of Bethlehem were only ten or twelve years old, they were taught to care for the sheep and cattle. By the time they were fourteen or fifteen, they could tend them as well as the men.

David had gone into the fields with the men and had learned how to care for the sheep.

As soon as he was old enough, he took the flocks out every day to the hillsides.

He was a very careful shepherd; if a little lamb was hurt, he would hold it tenderly in his arms and try to make it feel better.

If any of the sheep wandered away, David would go and bring them back.

He was careful to lead his sheep where the pastures were fresh and green. He was careful to take them beside the clear, still waters, for he knew that sheep do not like the rushing, roaring water. And he was just as kind to them, as if they had been people, instead of animals.

David gave names to all of his sheep and every morning he would stand at the door of the sheep-fold, and call each one of them.

Every evening, when the time came to go home, he would call them again and they would come running to his side.

Sometimes a little lamb, that had wandered away, would not hear his voice.

David would leave all of the other sheep, to hunt for the missing one. When he found it, he would carry the little lamb in his arms, back to the fold.

David's sheep knew his voice and would come when he called, but they would not obey a stranger.

David would sit on a rock and watch them as they nibbled grass.

Sometimes he would play on his harp, which he nearly always carried to the field with him.

When the sheep were not hungry, they would often lie at his feet, just as you see them in the picture.

Sometimes, David used to practice throwing at a mark with his sling-shot, but he kept close watch of his sheep all the while.

Once a bear broke into the flock and started away with a little lamb.

David killed the bear with a big stick and carried the little lamb back to its mother.

Another time a big lion broke in, and caught a little lamb.

Brave David seized him by the beard, killed him, and saved the little lamb.

David knew, that he could not have done these things, all by himself.

"It was God," he said, "who delivered me out of the paw of the lion and the bear."

When David grew to be a man, he often thought of his sheep and how he had taken care to lead them into green pastures and beside still waters.

"I am sure God loves his children, just as I love my sheep," he said to himself.

Then David wrote the beautiful Psalm, called the "Shepherd Psalm," that is used everywhere in the world.

This is just the way David wrote it:
> The Lord is my shepherd; I shall not want.
> He maketh me to lie down in green pastures;
> He leadeth me beside the still waters.
> He restoreth my soul;
> He leadeth me in the paths of righteousness for His name's sake.
> Yea, though I walk through the valley of the shadow of death,
> I will fear no evil; for Thou art with me;
> Thy rod and Thy staff they comfort me.
> Thou preparest a table before me in the presence of mine enemies;
> Thou anointest my head with oil;
> My cup runneth over.
> Surely goodness and mercy shall follow me all the days of my life;
> And I will dwell in the house of the Lord forever.

A SHEPHERD BOY AND A GIANT

AS David took care of his father's sheep day after day, he tried to do the things that would please his father, Jesse.

He pleased the Father in heaven, too, for God is always pleased when His children do right.

David liked to practice with his sling-shot, but he never thought that some day he would save his king's army by using it.

But he did, and this is the way it happened; three of his brothers were in the king's army.

One day as David was watching his sheep, his father sent a servant to ask him to come to the house.

Of course David went right home, to see what his father wanted, and when he reached home, Jesse asked him if he would go up to the king's army and take some food to his brothers.

David was about fifteen or sixteen years old and, you may be sure, he was glad and anxious to go.

The father began to pack some things which he wished David to take,—there was a lot of parched corn and barley cakes and cheese.

It was about fifteen miles to the camp and David went happily on his journey.

He thought, "How glad the boys will be to get this nice food from home, and they will be glad to give this cheese to their captain."

David walked happily away, but there was not much happiness in the king's army. It was all trouble there.

The army of King Saul of Israel, was camped on a long chain of hills. Across a little valley was another row of hills, and here was the army of their enemy, the Philistines.

When King Saul's men looked across this valley, their eyes met a terrible sight.

It was a great giant, covered from head to foot with metal armor.

The giant, whose name was Goliath, came out of his tent, and walked up and down the valley, making fun of King Saul's men.

He laughed at them and dared them to come and fight him.

"Have you anyone that will come and fight me?" he sneered. But the king's men were all afraid; there was not one who would say, "I will go and fight him."

Every day, for a long time, the old giant had been daring King Saul's men to send out a man.

Every day the king had hoped, that some one of his men, would be brave enough to go down into the valley and meet the giant. But no one had dared, and the king and his men were at their wits' end, when one day a boy came into camp.

He was David, the young shepherd boy, son of Jesse, and he had brought some presents, of parched corn and barley loaves for his older brothers in the king's army. After he had delivered the presents, some of the men showed David the old giant, that was causing them so much trouble.

They told him that he had been walking up and down the valley, every morning and evening for forty days, and that there was no one brave enough to fight him.

Very quickly David said, "I would not be afraid." Someone brought the word to the king.

When King Saul saw David, he said, "Why, you are not able to fight this Philistine. You are just a youth, and he is a man of war."

But David looked at the king and said, "King Saul, once when I was keeping my father's sheep, a lion broke into the flock and took a lamb, and I went after him, and hit him and killed him.

"And once, King Saul, a bear broke into the flock and took a lamb, and I killed him, too.

"O King, it was Jehovah that delivered me out of the paw of the lion and the bear, and He will deliver me from that man."

Then King Saul said to David, "Go, and Jehovah be with thee."

The king took off his own armor and put it on David. It was so heavy that David said, "I cannot go with these, for I have not proved them."

He knew that he would fight better, if he went in his everyday clothing.

Then David took his little sling in one hand and a staff in the other, and started down the hillside.

Everybody was watching him. They saw David stoop and pick up five smooth stones from the brook and drop them in the wallet which hung by his side.

He went on, and the old giant came out to meet him.

"Do you think I'm a dog, that you come here to fight me with a staff in your hand?" mocked Goliath.

He said very many ugly things to David, but the shepherd boy paid no attention.

He looked at Goliath and said, "You come to me with a sword, a spear, and a shield, but I come to you in the name of Jehovah of hosts."

David took just one little stone from the wallet by his side and put it in his sling.

He gave the sling a whirl and let the stone fly, and it struck the giant in the middle of the forehead and he fell down dead.

When the Philistines saw that their great leader was dead they turned and fled.

King Saul's army shouted and cheered, when they knew that a boy had saved their country.

They ran down the hill and chased the Philistines away.

David went back to the king's army and everybody thought he had done a wonderful thing.

"Whose son art thou, my young man?" asked the king. David answered, "I am the son of thy servant, Jesse, the Bethlehemite."

King Saul was so grateful to David, that he asked him to come and live in his palace.

TWO GOOD FRIENDS

IT was on the day that David killed the giant Goliath, that the shepherd boy and King Saul's son, Prince Jonathan, saw each other for the first time.

While the king was talking with David in his tent, Prince Jonathan took off his own beautiful coat and put it around the other lad's shoulders.

As soon as the two young men had looked into each other's eyes, they knew that they were going to be the closest of friends.

David was soon to find out, that he had need of Jonathan's friendship.

Although King Saul had invited David to come and live in his palace, he soon wanted him out of the way. He was really jealous because the people so dearly loved this young man, who had saved them from the Philistines.

One day when King Saul and David were returning from battle, crowds of people came out to greet them with music.

One song in particular made King Saul very angry. It was:
"Saul hath slain his thousands,
And David his ten thousands."

"O," said the king, "they are singing that I have slain thousands! And David has slain ten thousands!

"There is nothing more that he can do now, but to take the kingdom away from me, and I'll watch that he doesn't do that."

David did not know that King Saul was angry with him, but the next day while he was playing on his harp to entertain the king, Saul reached for his spear and threw it straight at David.

Fortunately the spear missed him and stuck in the wall.

Jonathan knew that his father meant harm to David, and he thought he ought to warn his friend.

So Jonathan asked David to take a long walk with him, out into the fields.

"David," he said, "my father is trying to kill you and I want you to stay out of his way.

"Hide here in the field and I will go back to the palace, and see how he feels toward you; if he is still angry, I will come back here and let you know.

"You must stay hidden, for we will both have to be very careful that no one sees us.

"I will bring a boy with me to gather up the arrows, as I practice shooting, and I will shoot toward the place where you are hiding.

"If I find out that my father is not going to hurt you, I will call to the boy and say, 'Behold, the arrows are on this side of thee.'

"But if I say, 'Behold, the arrows are beyond thee,' then you will know that he is still angry and that you must get away just as fast as you can."

When Jonathan went back to the palace, he found that his father was in a very bad mood. So after two days he took a boy and went back to the field.

David listened anxiously to hear what Jonathan would say when he shot the arrows, and this is what he heard: "Run, boy, the arrow is beyond thee."

Then he heard Jonathan say, "Make speed, haste, stay not."

The boy did not know that Jonathan meant these words for someone else, but David knew, and just as soon as Jonathan sent the boy home, he came out from his hiding place.

Then these two dear friends, the shepherd boy and the prince, put their arms around each other and cried.

Each promised that he would never forget the other and would pray for him always and care for any of his family.

They kissed each other goodbye and David went away off into a distant land, and Jonathan returned to his father's palace.

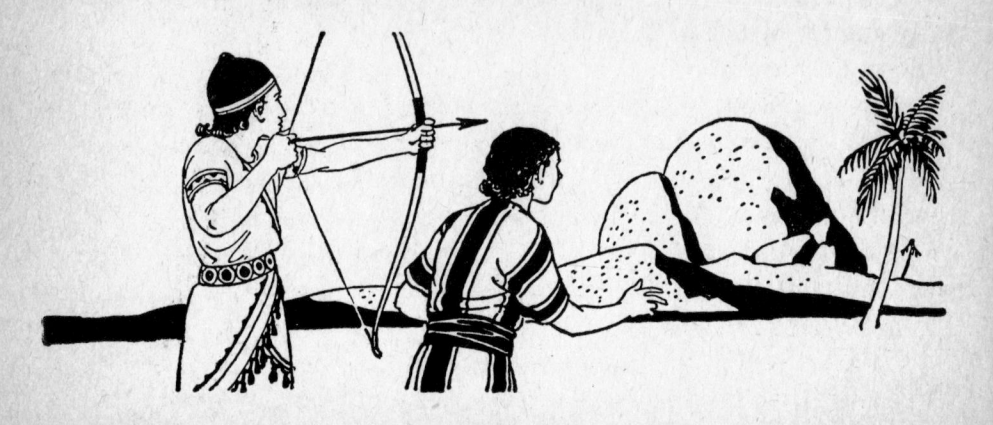

A KING AND A LAME PRINCE

KING Saul and his son, Jonathan, were both killed in battle, and David became the king of the Children of Israel.

Jonathan had a little son, who was five years old when his father was killed.

When the news came that Jonathan had been killed, the little boy's nurse was afraid that the soldiers would come and get him, too.

She took the little boy up in her arms and as she was running away she let him fall.

He grew up to manhood lame in both feet and could not be cured.

One day King David was thinking about his dear friend, Jonathan, and grieving that such a good man had to be killed in battle.

He thought about the time when he had first met Jonathan, after the death of the old giant, Goliath.

He thought about the time, out in the field, when they had told each other that they would always pray for one another, and that they would be kind to anyone in their families.

"I wonder if Jonathan had any children," said David to himself. "If he did, I must keep my word to love and care for them."

King David had an old servant, Ziba, who he thought might know all about Jonathan's family.

He sent for Ziba, and asked him if any of Saul's family were living.

"Jonathan hath yet a son who is lame on his feet. He hath been lame ever since he was a little boy," answered Ziba.

Then David asked Ziba all about this son of Jonathan's and the old servant told him how he came to be lame, and everything else that he knew about him.

It did not take David very long to make up his mind, what he would do for Jonathan's son.

"Ziba," he said, "I am going to have him come and live in the palace; will you bring him to me?"

Mephibosheth, Jonathan's son, could hardly believe that the king had sent for him.

He got ready to go over to the palace with Ziba and when the two went into King David's presence, they bowed very low.

Ziba said, "O king, this is Jonathan's son, Mephibosheth," then he left the king and the lame prince to talk together.

Mephibosheth knelt before King David, and the king said to

him kindly, "Don't be afraid, for I will surely show thee kindness for Jonathan, thy father's sake, and you shall live in the palace all of your life."

The lame man looked at King David and said, "Why is it that you want to help so poor a creature as I?"

Then the king told this son of Jonathan's about their great friendship for each other.

"Mephibosheth," he said, "why shouldn't I help you? Your father saved my life and he was my best friend, I am glad to have the chance to do something for you."

It made the lame man very happy, indeed, to have the king treat him so kindly, and he gladly went to the palace to live.

Mephibosheth had a little son of his own and he, too, went to the king's palace.

King David called his servant again and said, "Now, Ziba, I have given back to Jonathan's son all the land that belonged to him, and I want you to take your sons and your servants, and till the ground and raise all that you can for Mephibosheth and his family."

Ziba had fifteen sons, and twenty servants and they all went out and planted the grain and did as the king had asked.

The lame prince and his son lived in the palace and ate at the same table with King David, as long as they lived.

KING SOLOMON BUILDS A BEAUTIFUL TEMPLE

KING David of Israel lived in a beautiful palace. It was built of the finest of wood and richly furnished.

One day, as he was sitting in this costly palace, he thought of the house where the people went to worship God.

"Here am I," said he, "in a house made of cedar, and the ark of God rests in a house made of curtains."

Then a great longing came to David, to build a temple for God's worship, a temple that should be the very finest building in the whole world.

Sometimes King David was not sure that the plans he had in mind would please God. Then he would tell them to the great prophet Nathan and Nathan would bring him an answer from God.

So now he sent for Nathan and told him, how much he wanted to build a beautiful house for God.

That night, Nathan told God David's wish, and God sent a message back to the king that Solomon, David's son, was to build the temple and not David himself.

This was the beautiful message that Nathan carried to David, from the Father in heaven: "I shall not forget thee; when I took thee from the sheep-cote, from following the sheep, it was to make thee a prince over my people;

"And I have been with thee at all times, and have kept thee from thine enemies, and I will make thee a great name."

When God spoke of Solomon, He said, "I will be his father, and he shall be my son; my loving-kindness shall not depart from him."

When the king heard God's message, he went into a room by himself to pray.

He prayed a long, long time, and almost every word of his prayer was one of thanksgiving.

"O, Jehovah," he prayed, "there is none like thee, neither is there any God beside thee."

David was glad that God had chosen his son, Solomon, to build the temple and he planned to help in every way that he could.

He gathered together gold and silver and precious stones, and a great deal of money.

When Solomon grew older, David talked with him about the time when he should build the great temple.

He told him all about the plans that God had made, and said, "Be thou strong, and show thyself a man, and walk in the way of Jehovah, thy God."

At last when King David's work on earth was done he died, and his son, Solomon became king.

Solomon was a good, wise king and tried to obey, all the commands of David his father.

He soon began his plans for the building of God's house.

He sent for the best workmen that could be found anywhere. He needed many, for there was a great deal of work to be done.

The top of a great mountain had to be cut away, so that the temple could stand upon it, and the sides had to be walled up, so that it would be very strong.

Huge rocks had to be wedged into the side of the mountain, so that it would not crumble away.

Away to the north there were great forests of cedar, and the biggest and strongest of these had to be cut down and brought many miles.

Men who were skillful in making ornaments of gold and silver and iron and brass were needed, as well as weavers of the finest of linen cloth, for the curtains of the temple.

It took a long, long time, to build this wonderful temple.

The men worked over seven and one-half years in all, but they worked gladly, because they were building a house for God's worship.

And when at last the temple was finished, it was very, very beautiful.

On either side of the great shining altar, stood five tall candlesticks of pure gold.

The inside doors were covered with gold and many precious stones sparkled from the walls.

King Solomon asked all the people of the whole country to come to the temple, to worship God on the very first day that it was open.

It was a dazzling sight when the king and five-hundred guards, each carrying a golden shield, came marching into the temple.

The Priests took up the ark and carried it to its place in the inner room of the temple, under the wings of the two golden winged cherubims.

Great bands of musicians in snowy white robes, stood on either side of the altar.

God in heaven must have been pleased, when He heard all the people singing one of the beautiful songs of King David: "O, give thanks unto the Lord, for he is good; for his loving-kindness endureth forever."

God wanted the people to know that He was pleased and accepted their thanks, so He sent a sign to them. A great cloud seemed to fill the temple, and the people understood what it meant.

Then King Solomon stood with lifted hands and prayed, thanking God for all His goodness to His people, and promising that they would always be faithful to Him.

After the prayer was over, the king turned to the people, and told them to live always very close to God, then he said, "Jehovah, our God, be with us, as He was with our fathers."

The people had seven days of thanksgiving and prayer and then they went to their homes.

HOW GOD TOOK CARE OF ELIJAH

ONCE there was a great prophet named Elijah.
Elijah carried God's messages to the people. Sometimes he had pleasant messages to carry, but when the people had been wicked, the messages were sad.

At one time, the king of the people of Israel, Ahab, went into a heathen country and married a woman who worshipped idols.

When she came to live in Ahab's country, she tried to make his people worship idols, too. Many of them forgot their true Father in heaven, and prayed to an idol called Baal.

Ahab, the king, to please his wife, worshipped Baal also. He did more evil things in the sight of God than any king who had ever lived in Israel.

One day God called Elijah and gave him this message for wicked King Ahab.

"As the Lord God of Israel liveth, before whom I stand, there shall not be dew nor rains these years, but according to my word."

The king was so angry that he tried to take Elijah's life, but the Father in heaven would let no harm come to the good prophet.

He said to him, "Elijah, go from here, turn to the eastward, and hide thyself by the Brook Cherith.

"And it shall be that thou shalt drink of the brook; and I have told the ravens to feed thee there."

Elijah went to the Brook Cherith, and every morning the ravens brought bread and meat to him.

The ravens came every evening, too, with more food for Elijah.

For nearly three years the great prophet lived in this way, until there came a day when there was no more water in the brook.

Then God said to Elijah, "Elijah, arise, get thee to Zarephath and dwell there. I have told a widow woman there to care for thee."

So Elijah set out for Zarephath. There he saw a woman gathering sticks, and asked her if she would bring him a drink of water.

As the woman started for the water, Elijah called after her, "Bring me, I pray thee, a morsel of bread in thy hand."

"I haven't a cake," said the woman, "I have nothing but a handful of meal and a little oil in a cruse: and I am gathering two sticks that I may go in and dress it for me and my son, that we may eat it and die."

Then Elijah told her not to be afraid and he said, "Go and do as you have said; but make me a little cake first, and after that, make for yourself and son."

He then told her that God had promised: "The jar of meal shall not waste, neither shall the cruse of oil fail, until the day that the Lord sendeth rain upon the earth."

A wonderful thing happened in the widow woman's home. Every time she looked into the jar of meal, she found just as much as there had been before, and every time she went to the cruse of oil, she found just as much as there had been!

While Elijah was staying in the widow's home, a great sorrow came to the poor woman.

Her son, the only child she had, became so ill that he died.

The poor woman was very sad indeed, but Elijah took the boy away from her, and carried him up-stairs to the room in which he himself had slept, and laid him upon his own bed.

Then Elijah prayed, "O Lord, my God, I pray thee, let this child's soul come into him again."

God heard Elijah's prayer and life came back to the little boy.

"Now I know that thou art a prophet, sent from God," the happy and grateful mother cried out to Elijah.

After Elijah had been a prophet for many long years, God told him that it was time for him to rest.

"Elijah, there will be a new prophet in your place, and his name is Elisha," he said.

Elijah was walking with Elisha one day, out by the river Jordan.

He turned to the young man and said, "Elisha, is there anything you would like to have me do for you before I go away?"

"Only this," Elisha answered, "help me to be as good as you have been."

Then Elijah said, "I cannot do these things of myself, but God will make a sign to you, Elisha, that if you see me when I am taken from you, it shall be so."

After a little while, a brilliant light shone in the sky. "There appeared a chariot of fire, and horses of fire, and parted them both asunder; and Elijah went up by a whirlwind into Heaven."

Elisha saw the chariot and fire, and the good old prophet, as he went up, and he fell to the earth and cried, "My father, my father!"

Then Elisha picked up the mantle that had fallen from Elijah, and became the great prophet in Elijah's place.

A CAPTIVE MAID HELPS HER MASTER

ONCE there was a pretty little dark-eyed girl, who lived happily with her father and mother, in the city of Jerusalem.

One day soldiers from a heathen country came to her beautiful city. They tore down its walls; they spoiled the costly temple; and they took many of the people away with them as prisoners.

These soldiers did not stop with grown-up prisoners, but they took boys and girls, too, and this loving, dark-eyed girl was among them.

She had to walk many a long mile, before she reached the far away country, where she was to be a slave.

There everything was strange and new. How much she missed her dear father and mother! She had to try very hard to be brave.

The captain of the soldiers wanted someone to help his wife, and he took the little girl to his home.

The great captain's name was Naaman. He was very rich, but he was far from happy, for he had a terrible disease called leprosy.

Although Captain Naaman's people were sorry for him, they dared not go near enough to touch him. It was not safe to touch a leper.

Naaman's wife was very unhappy, for she knew that he could never be cured.

The little slave girl soon learned, what made her mistress look so sad.

How she wished she could help! And suddenly she thought about a great prophet, who lived in her own country.

She had heard many times about Elisha and the wonderful things he had done, and she was sure that if Captain Naaman would go to the land of Israel, her prophet, Elisha, could cure him.

One day, as the little girl waited on Naaman's wife, she said, "I would that my lord were with the prophet that is in Samaria."

Then she told the captain's wife about Elisha, and that she thought he could cure Naaman.

Naaman's wife sent for her husband at once, and as soon as he heard what the little slave girl had said about Elisha, he started for Samaria to see the great prophet.

And he took with him, many beautiful gifts for Elisha.

When he reached Elisha's country, he went to the king and told him his trouble.

"How can I cure a man with leprosy?" asked the king.

"Send for the prophet Elisha," said someone, "he will know what to do."

When the message reached Elisha, he sent this word back to the king: "Let the man now come to me, and he shall know, that there is a prophet in Israel."

With his horses and chariot the great captain drove up to the prophet's house. Elisha did not come to the door to meet him.

Instead he sent the captain this message: "Go and wash in the Jordan seven times, and thy flesh shall come again, and thou shalt be healed."

Naaman was angry that Elisha had not come out to meet him.

"The waters in my own country, are better than those of Israel. Why couldn't I wash at home?" he cried.

The captain turned and was going off in a rage, when one of the servants said, "Master, if the prophet had told you to do some great thing, you would have done it, wouldn't you? Now, why don't you do this little thing, which he has asked?"

The great captain saw that the servant was right, so he went to the Jordan river.

It was not clear and beautiful like his own rivers, but he would wash in it just the same.

He went down into the water, and dipped himself one, two, three times, and when he came up each time, the dreadful disease was still there.

He did not stop, but he dipped himself four, five, six, seven times just as Elisha had told him.

When he came up the seventh time, his flesh was as clean and pure as that of a little child.

He was cured of his leprosy! And you may be sure, that it was a happy man, who thanked Elisha and started back home.

When the great Naaman reached home, he thanked the little slave girl, too, who had helped him to find God's great prophet, Elisha.

A GUEST ROOM

AS Elisha went about his work, after he had become the great prophet in Israel, he often used to pass through a little village called Shunem.

In the village of Shunem, there lived a woman so helpful and kind that everybody there, called her a great woman.

Elisha and his servant often had to pass the woman's home, and one day she invited them in to rest a while, and to have dinner with her and her husband.

After that, Elisha and his servant often stopped to see these good people, and they had many pleasant talks together.

One day the woman said to her husband, "I am sure this man who passes here so often, is a good man going about God's work.

"He has nowhere to stay; let us build a little room for him, and put a table and a bed and a stool and a candlestick in it.

"And when he comes this way, he and his servant may go in there and rest as long as they like."

So the little room was built at once and neatly furnished.

The next time Elisha and his servant came along, the Shunammite called them in and showed them the new room, which her husband had built for them.

Elisha went in and rested there for a time, then he said to his servant, "Call the Shunammite." And when she came up to the room, they thanked her for all her kindness to them.

Elisha asked then, "Is there anything we can do for you? Would you like to have me speak to the king, or anyone else to do a favor for you?"

But the woman said, that she was content living there, among her own people in Shunem.

Elisha's servant said to him, "There is only one thing these people need. They have no son to make them happy."

Elisha prayed to God to send a little son to this home, and the prayer was answered.

The child grew up and in time he was old enough, to go into the fields with his father.

One day when he was in the field where the men were at work cutting the wheat, he suddenly began to cry, "O father, my head, my head!"

The father called a servant and said, "Carry the boy home to his mother."

The servant took the little boy home and put him on his mother's knee.

She held him until noon-time, trying to stop his pain, but she could not help him and after a while, the little fellow died in her arms.

At first, the mother did not know what to do. Then she said to herself, "I will take him up stairs to Elisha's room, and then I will go to his home, and tell him what has happened. Maybe he can help."

So she carried the little boy up stairs and laid him on the bed, in the prophet's room.

She closed the door behind her, and went quickly to the field where her husband was working, and asked him to send a servant to her with a mule.

Without stopping to tell her husband what was the matter, she started off on the mule for Elisha's home.

She urged the servant to drive fast, and not to stop for anything.

"Drive, and go forward;" she said, "slacken me not the riding, except as I bid thee," and on they went, as fast as they could for twelve miles.

Elisha saw her coming, and he wondered if anything was wrong.

"Yonder is the Shunammite;" he said to his servant, "run, I pray thee now, to meet her, and say unto her, 'Is it well with thee? Is it well with thy husband? Is it well with thy child?'"

The servant did as he was told.

"It is well," the woman answered the servant and she hurried past him to reach Elisha.

She fell down at his feet and began to talk about her little son.

Then Elisha knew what had happened. Giving his staff to his servant he sent him on ahead, telling him to place it upon the child's face.

The Shunammite was afraid then, that Elisha was not going with her, and that her little boy would not be healed.

"As the Lord liveth, and as thy soul liveth, I will not leave thee," she said to Elisha.

Elisha seeing what great faith the woman had in him, arose and went with her.

His servant had gone on to the house and had done just exactly, what Elisha had told him to do.

But he started back, and when he met Elisha and the woman, he said, "The child is not awakened."

When Elisha reached the house, he went to the room where the boy lay on the bed, and closed the door.

Elisha prayed to the Father in Heaven. Then he went up and "lay upon the little child, and put his mouth upon his mouth, and his eyes upon the boy's eyes, his hands upon the boy's hands, and the flesh of the little child grew warm."

Elisha left the room and walked to and fro, then he went back and stretched himself once more on the child. This time the little boy, sneezed seven times and opened his eyes.

The little fellow's mother was called at once and Elisha said to her, "Take up thy son."

Joyfully she poured out her thanks and fell down at Elisha's feet; then she took up her son and went out.

A LITTLE BOY KING

THERE lived at one time in the city of Jerusalem, a king who had a large family of sons.

Of course every one thought, that when this king died, one of his sons would take his place.

But the old king's mother, a very wicked woman named Athaliah, wanted to be queen herself.

"The king's sons shall all be destroyed," she said to herself, "and then I shall be the queen of this country."

So as soon as she heard that the king was dead, this wicked woman gave orders to have all his sons killed.

Now one of these sons was only a little baby. His aunt hoping to be able to save him, hid the baby and his nurse in a bed chamber. Athaliah did not find Baby Joash and so she thought that all her grandsons were dead.

The baby's aunt took him secretly to the temple, where the good priest, Jehoiada, lived, and this priest kept the little boy hidden away there for six years.

All this time wicked Athaliah ruled as queen.

One day, to her great surprise, she found out that she was not the queen after all.

When little Joash was seven years old, good Jehoiada made up his mind that he would tell the people, that all the king's sons were not dead.

He would show them the little boy who had been hidden away.

Jehoiada knew that everybody would be glad, for no one liked Athaliah.

One day he sent for the soldiers and the captains, to come to the temple and brought the little king out before them!

"Joash is the son of the king," Jehoiada said to them, "we have kept him hidden so that the queen could not get him; he is seven years old now, and it is time for you to know that you still have a king."

How surprised and how glad they were!

Then the good priest planned with the soldiers, that they should guard Joash, until the time when he should be made king before all the people.

King David's spears and shields had all been kept in the temple, and Jehoiada brought them out and gave them to the captains.

When the people all came together, these captains, with their spears and shields, formed a great guard for the little king, and stood around the temple from one side to the other.

Then Jehoiada brought Joash out again, and put the gold crown upon his head.

The people all clapped their hands and shouted, "Long live the king! Long live the king!"

The old queen heard the noise; she hurried to the temple and saw little Joash. When she heard the men shout, "Long live the king!" she was so angry that she tore her clothing and cried out, "Treason, treason!"

Jehoiada was afraid that the men might kill her there in the temple, so he asked them to take her away.

From that day, this little boy only seven years old, became the king. He was of course too young to know how to rule, but he prayed to God every day for help, and the good priest Jehoiada was ever at his side.

Joash always tried to be a good ruler. When he was a little older he saw that parts of the temple needed mending. He told Jehoiada to have the men bring money and drop it in a chest.

"Keep the money there until there is enough to put the temple in order," he said to Jehoiada.

As soon as there was enough money in the chest, it was counted and given to the carpenters, the masons, and the other workmen to buy timber and stone and whatever was needed.

The people were very glad, that Joash had helped them make the temple like new.

Joash was a good king of Judah, and reigned in Jerusalem for many, many years.

AT SCHOOL IN A KING'S PALACE

THE beautiful city of Jerusalem, was very dear to the hearts of the people of Israel.

It was, therefore, a very sad time for them, when a heathen king from a far away land, sent his soldiers against Jerusalem.

They tore down the walls and rushed into the city.

They even broke into the temple that King Solomon had built and carried away the beautiful golden candlesticks, the vessels of gold, silver and brass, and what they could not carry off, they pulled down and trampled upon.

Many of the people of Israel were killed, too, by the heathen soldiers and others were sent off as captives to their own city of Babylon.

They chose the strongest, the handsomest and the most quick-witted of the Jewish boys and girls and grown-up men and women, thinking they would make the best slaves.

Among the captives were four bright, sturdy boys called Daniel, Shadrach, Meshach, and Abednego.

The Bible does not tell us whether these boys had been friends in

Jerusalem, but we do know that when they reached the city of Babylon, they were close companions in the king's palace.

They were all four very fine, brave boys, but Daniel was the one who took the lead. He often spoke to the other three about the old home in Jerusalem, and especially of the beautiful temple in which they all used to worship God, and of the shameful way the heathen soldiers had treated it.

As they walked together, they would say, "But there is nothing that will keep us from worshipping our God in Heaven. We will always be true to him."

They made up their minds, also, that they would always remember the lessons, which their fathers and mothers had taught them in their old home.

One day King Nebuchadnezzar ordered, that some of the captive boys be brought before him.

And so it happened that Daniel, Shadrach, Meshach, and Abednego were among the number.

He was very much pleased with these strong, clear-eyed boys.

"Feed these boys with the best food—the same kind of food that

I eat, and give them wine to drink so that they may become fair," he ordered his steward.

The four boys did not want to injure themselves, by eating the king's rich food and by drinking his wine.

When they refused it, the king's steward scarcely knew what to do. He was afraid these boys would not look as strong and healthy as the others, when they were next brought before the king, and he would be blamed and perhaps, punished.

But the boys begged, "O, but just try us for ten days, please; do not make us eat the king's food and do not make us drink his wine.

"Give us plain food to eat and water to drink and at the end of ten days we shall be as strong as the other boys. Do give us a trial."

Now the king's steward had found the boys so trustworthy and they were so much in earnest, that at last he gave in.

When the ten days were up, the king's steward called the boys before him and looked them over.

He was pleased to find that they were stronger and fairer in every way, than the other boys who had taken the king's food and wine.

From that time on the steward gave them plain food and water, for he had made up his mind that simple meals, were best for growing boys.

For three years these four friends, Daniel, Shadrach, Meshach, and Abednego, went to school with the other boys in the palace of King Nebuchadnezzar.

They had many things to learn; first of all to serve the king in every way.

The king's steward was their teacher.

At the end of three years, the four companions were called before the king. He was so pleased with them, that he asked them to stay in his palace and be his helpers all the time.

More than the king, God in Heaven was pleased with the boys and blessed them in every way.

A FIERY FURNACE

DANIEL, Shadrach, Meshach and Abednego were the Jewish boys who lived in the king's palace, and he soon learned to love them very much.

He wanted them to stay with him always, for he knew he could trust them.

They were his officers for a great many years.

He had been so pleased with Daniel, that he had made him a great ruler, in the city of Babylon.

Shadrach, Meshach and Abednego he had kept with him, and they were always true to his commands.

In their old home at Jerusalem, these boys had been taught never to do anything wrong.

They had been taught, that God in Heaven was the true God and that they never should worship idols.

A long time before this story happened, God had said to His people, "Thou shalt have no other gods before me," and these boys remembered that command.

[111]

The king, Nebuchadnezzar, did not believe in God. He was what people call a heathen. That means he worshipped idols.

The king thought that because he was so powerful, he should build a great idol for his people to worship.

So he set to work to build an idol, that was finer than any of the other idols had ever been.

It took a long time and a great many workmen, to make this big idol out of the finest gold.

At last it was finished, a great golden image, ninety feet high, and worth a great deal of money.

King Nebuchadnezzar was very proud when the idol was finished, and he wanted all the people to come and worship it.

He sent word to all the rulers and the officers in his kingdom to go to the plain of Dura, just outside the city of Babylon. Here was where the idol had been set up.

He asked for all the bands of music in his kingdom, and commanded that when the people heard the sound of the flute, the cornet or harp they should fall down and worship the idol.

"If there be anyone that will not fall down and worship this idol, he shall be cast into a fiery furnace," was the king's order.

Shadrach, Meshach and Abednego were among the officers, who were commanded to do that.

It was a hard test for them, because the king had been very kind to them.

They said to each other, "We cannot do this, for the great God in Heaven is the King above all gods, and Him only will we serve."

They knew that the king's command would be kept, if they did not worship the great golden image.

They were strong, fearless men and felt that even if they were cast into the fiery furnace, God in Heaven would take care of them.

All at once came the sound of music, the notes of the flute, the cornet, the harp and other instruments; the people fell on their faces before the great image.

Crowds and crowds of them bowed down, until only three men were left standing. They were Shadrach, Meshach and Abednego.

Word soon came to the king, that these three men would not bow down and worship his idol.

Angrily he sent for the three men and asked why they did not bow down.

Then remembering they were his trusted officers, he gave them another chance.

"Now when you hear the sound of music, if you will bow down and worship this image which I have made, it is well," said the king.

"If you worship not, you shall be cast in the midst of a burning, fiery furnace, and who is that God who shall deliver you out of my hands?"

The three brave men answered, "We have no need to answer thee in this matter.

"If it be so, our God, whom we serve, is able to deliver us from the burning, fiery furnace; and he will deliver us out of thy hands, O King.

"But if not, be it known unto thee, O King, that we will not serve thy gods, nor worship the golden image which thou hast set up."

The king was very angry indeed and told men to heat the furnace, seven times hotter than it had ever been before.

Then he ordered strong men to bind Shadrach, Meshach and Abednego, and throw them into the furnace.

The king's men seized the three brave men and without taking off their clothes, they bound their hands and feet, so they could not move, and cast them into the midst of the roaring furnace.

As the king stood watching the furnace, instead of three men he saw four, among the flames, and they were not bound at all! They were not even hurt.

They were walking around and the king was so astonished, he did not know what to do.

He called some of his men and in great surprise he asked, "Did we not cast three men into the fire?" And they answered, "True, O King."

And the king said, "Lo, I see four men loose, walking in the midst of the fire and they have no hurt; and the form of the fourth is like the Son of God."

Then the king walked up to the mouth of the furnace and called the three men by name, "Shadrach, Meshach and Abednego, come forth."

And they came forth out of the fire, and there was not even the smell of fire about them,—not a hair on their heads had been harmed.

King Nebuchadnezzar sent out word to all his people, telling them that no one in all that country, should speak a word against the God of these men.

He said, "For there is no other God able to deliver after this sort."

And the king gave high positions to these three brave men.

IN A DEN OF LIONS

AFTER King Nebuchadnezzar and his son died, a new king, by the name of Darius, ruled the people.

King Darius soon found out that Daniel, one of the captive lads from Jerusalem, who had grown up in the palace, was the finest spirited and most trustworthy of all his officers. He therefore gave Daniel the highest position in the kingdom.

Now the other officers were jealous and angry that a man from another land, should be set above them. They made up their minds to get rid of him.

They tried their best to find some fault with the way Daniel did his work, so that they might complain to the king about him. But Daniel was a very faithful officer and did exactly as the king ordered.

They could find no fault with him. At last, however, they thought of a way in which they might make trouble for Daniel with the king: Daniel worshipped God and they worshipped idols.

They planned to go before King Darius and make him think, he was greater than Daniel's God.

So one day they marched in and bowed low before the king, "O

[116]

king," they begged, "make a law that whosoever shall ask anything of anyone but you for thirty days, shall be cast into a den of lions."

The king gladly made the law, for he liked having everybody bow to him.

He knew nothing of Daniel's God, so he never once thought that his officers were really setting a trap, in which to catch Daniel.

The king sent word about the new law to all the people, saying:

"I have just signed a new law, that if anyone in this kingdom prays to any God or man, except myself, for thirty days, he shall be cast into a den of lions."

Daniel, of course, heard of the law, but he would not stop praying to God in heaven. He knew that God was greater than any king who was on earth, and he knew, too, that his God would take care of him.

Daniel had always prayed three times a day. Morning, noon and evening he would stop his work and go to a window, a window that opened east toward his dear old home in Jerusalem, and there he would kneel down and pray.

Daniel was never ashamed to be seen praying and now he prayed as usual.

The evil men were spying on him and when they saw Daniel on his knees, and heard his words of prayer, they said, "Now is our chance."

They hurried to the king. "O king," they said, "didn't you make a law that anyone who prayed to any God, or man besides yourself, should be cast into a den of lions?"

The king answered that he had and that a law once made, could not be changed.

Then they said, "This man Daniel, one of the captives from Jerusalem, pays no heed to you or your law, but prays three times a day without regard to your word."

The king was very sorry to hear these words. He tried all day to think of some way to free Daniel, but the jealous officers would not listen.

There was nothing left for him to do, but to have Daniel cast into the den of lions.

"Your God will take care of you, Daniel," said King Darius to Daniel, before he was put into the den.

So Daniel was put into the den with the lions.

Then the opening to the den was filled with a great stone, which was sealed with the king's own seal ring and those of his nobles, to make sure that no one would let Daniel out.

After that the king went back to his palace, but he felt so sorry for Daniel that he could not sleep. He could only think about Daniel, his good, trusty helper.

Very, very early the next morning, the king went over to the den of lions.

When he came near, he cried out in a sad voice, "O Daniel! Daniel! Did your God take care of you?"

The king was almost afraid to speak, for he thought he would never hear Daniel's voice again.

But Daniel answered, "O king, live forever. My God hath sent His angels and has shut the lions' mouths, and they have not hurt me."

The king was so happy to hear Daniel's voice. He asked his men to take Daniel, up out of the den and they soon saw he had not been hurt at all, for he had trusted in God.

Then King Darius wrote to all the people and told them the story of Daniel, and asked them to trust in Daniel's God.

A QUEEN WHO SAVED HER PEOPLE

ONCE in the far away country of Persia, there lived a very beautiful young girl whose name was Esther.

She had neither father nor mother and had been adopted by her cousin, Mordecai.

Mordecai was not a Persian.

His home had been in Jerusalem, and he had been taken captive over to Babylon, just as Daniel had been.

Mordecai was like Daniel in another way, too; he was very noble and courageous.

He held a very high place in the king's court, and the king knew that he could trust him.

After many years a new king, whose name was Xerxes, was on the throne in Persia, and he wanted a lovely new queen to reign with him.

Some of the king's nobles advised him, to invite all the beautiful girls that he could find, and maybe there would be one among them who could be the queen.

When Mordecai heard this news, he wanted Esther to go before the king, with all the other beautiful girls.

Esther said to herself, "The king will never look at me."

"My dress is not beautiful and I have no jewels, like the other girls."

But King Xerxes *did* look at Esther; he saw how gentle and kind she was, and when he heard her soft, low voice, he chose her to be the queen.

She was very much surprised and her cousin, Mordecai, was pleased.

Now there was, in the king's court, a man whose name was Haman.

Haman was very jealous of Mordecai, because the king favored him, and he made up his mind to do Mordecai harm.

He knew that Mordecai was a Jew, so he decided to ask the king, to drive all the Jewish people out of his kingdom, or to kill them.

The wicked Haman went before the king with these words, "O king, in your kingdom is a race of people who refuse to obey your laws; you ought not to allow this, and they should be destroyed."

The king never stopped to think, how many Jewish people there were, nor how many of them were his own good friends.

He did not even know that his own sweet wife, Esther, was a Jewess, so he made the law that they should all be destroyed.

The word was sent out all over the kingdom, that on a certain day, all the Jewish people, men, women and children, should be put to death.

It was sad news to Mordecai; sad news to almost everyone, except the wicked Haman.

Mordecai and all the Jewish people, mourned and fasted and prayed.

The beautiful queen, Esther, saw her cousin as he came to the gate, and she knew that something was very wrong, so she sent a servant to see what was the matter.

When the servant went to Mordecai, that good man told him what had happened.

Mordecai gave the servant a paper for the queen, telling what Haman had done.

"Take this to the queen," said he, "and tell her, that she must ask the king to save her people."

Queen Esther sent this message back to Mordecai, "I cannot go before the king unless he asks for me, for whoever does this may be put to death, and I have not been called in thirty days."

His answer was, "Esther, do not care for yourself, because if all the Jews are put to death, you will perish with them."

Poor Queen Esther did not know what to do.

She wondered if the king would be glad to have her come in, or if he would be angry, but at last she made up her mind to go before him.

She sent her servant back to tell Mordecai, to call all of the Jewish people of the city together and to ask them to pray for her.

"I will not eat anything for three days, night nor day, and my maidens will not eat anything, and I will go in before the king, and if I perish, I perish," she said.

On the third day, the people were still praying and fasting, and the queen dressed herself in her most beautiful robes and went and stood where the king might see her.

The king knew that she would not come, unless there was something that she wanted very, very much, and he held out his golden scepter to her, as a sign that she was welcome.

King Xerxes looked at her and asked, "Queen Esther, what wilt thou? What is thy request? It shall be given you, to the half of my kingdom."

Then the queen asked him, if he would come to a great feast, which she had prepared for him, and bring Haman with him.

The king kindly went to the feast and took Haman with him. In the very midst of it, the king asked Queen Esther once more, what it was she wished and promised again to grant it.

Then the queen told the king what had happened.

She told him, that she herself belonged to the Jewish people, and asked him not to kill them.

King Xerxes was very sorry then, that he had signed the law that all the Jewish people should be put to death, and he was so angry at Haman, that he caused him to be hanged.

He let Mordecai and all the Jewish people go free, and was just as kind to them as he had been before.

The people never forgot, that they owed their lives to Esther's bravery.

S
001.4
F
c.2

Faris, Lillie A
Old Testament stories

DATE DUE		
FEB 4 '84		
MAY 28 '85		
JUN		
DEC 13 '90		

BETH HILLEL LIBRARY
WILMETTE, ILLINOIS

WITHDRAWN